The Christmas Gift
That Lasts A Lifetime

BOB PRYCE
&
ROBYN PRICE

Illustrated by
ROBYN PRICE

The Christmas Gift That Lasts A Lifetime

Robert Charles Price (pseudonym – Bob Pryce)
Robyn Marie Price

Library of Congress Control Number: 2002094562

ISBN 0-9675628-2-1

First Edition

Printed in the United States of America

Illustrations: Robyn Marie Price

If unavailable in local bookstores, additional copies of this and other publications by Bob Pryce may be purchased by writing to the address below.

Acknowledgments

My inspiration in writing this book comes from a supportive loving family. No father could have a better gift than to be able to create a book with his daughter.

I am deeply thankful to my wonderful parents who were always there to check each word in the progression of the book.

I would like to give a special heartfelt thanks to my son, Bobby, for photographing Robyn and me. Special thanks to Kumar Persad of Tri-State Litho Book Printing for spending time answering my many questions, and Cherie Kocsis for the excellent cover design.

Special thanks to George Flynn, a close friend, who helped edit the manuscript, and kept encouraging Robyn and me to have this book published.

This book is for

my extraordinarily wonderful wife, Nancy,
who has always given me the strength
to follow my dreams.

my four children,
Robyn, Bobby, Kenny and Kristen

my parents, Bob and Carol.

my brother, Jon, and my nephew, Alex.

in memory of
Danae, my best friend, and all the "good times"
we shared, love Robyn.

Chapter 1

Marie looked out her bedroom window and smiled while she watched the snow cascade to earth. Her younger brother Charlie peeked his head into her room and laughed. "Hey, Marie, whatcha looking at that is making you smile?" Marie turned around and laughed, "Just thinking about the time you tried to jump over a barrel while ice skating last week."

Charlie chuckled, "It beats the time you believed we would find a million dollars at the bottom of that hole over by the dump down the street."

Charlie left her room and went out to play. Marie sat there thinking about what Charlie had just said. It was kind of silly of me to think we would find a million dollars down by the dump. Marie scraped a little more ice off the inside of her window and continued to watch the snow fall.

The phone rang, and Marie turned and ran down the stairs to answer it. It was Charlie's friend Alex, from school. "Hi, is Charlie in?"

Marie looked out the window, "Alex, wait just a minute, I see him in the back yard."

Charlie heard Marie yell out to him that he had a phone call. As Charlie walked into the house, he asked who was on the phone. "It's your friend Alex," said Marie.

A frown came over Charlie's face. "Just tell him I'm not in," lied Charlie.

Marie was puzzled. This wasn't like her brother. Charlie was by far the most caring compassionate person she knew. He had the biggest heart of anyone she ever met. Marie picked up the phone and said, "Alex, can Charlie call you back?"

"Sure," replied Alex.

Marie looked at Charlie. "What was that all

about?"

"I don't want to talk about it," yelled Charlie.

Marie stared at Charlie and noticed the tears welling up. "What's wrong, Charlie?"

Charlie started to wipe the tears away. Fighting back more tears, he began to tell Marie why he didn't want to talk to Alex.

Charlie explained to Marie how Alex's family lives in a big beautiful home on the other side of town. Alex was calling to see if he could come over here to play tomorrow. Charlie began to cry again. "How can I have him over here to play? Our house is small and drafty. We don't even have heat upstairs in the bedrooms."

Slowly Marie went over to Charlie and gave him a big hug. "Charlie, you have nothing to be ashamed of."

"Yea sure, look at our house and look at the town dump down the road," cried Charlie.

"How can I let my friend Alex see where I live? He would never want to be my friend again."

Marie knew exactly what Charlie was feeling. She too had similar feelings in the past.

Chapter 2

The phone was ringing downstairs in the study. Alex turned around in his chair to answer it.

"Hi Alex, this is Charlie. I'm sorry I couldn't talk to you earlier. I was busy outside working on some things for my mom. I won't be able to have you over tomorrow to play."

Alex took a deep breath. At the instant the only thought he had was that Charlie was blowing him off. But as he listened, he could tell that Charlie was upset that he couldn't have him over. "Is everything alright?" inquired Alex.

Charlie hesitated before speaking. No, everything is not ok, thought Charlie. But instead in a trembling voice he said, "I have to do chores tomorrow around the house. Maybe when I'm done I can ride my bike over to your house?"

"That will be great. Do you think you could stay for dinner after we play?" asked Alex.

"I don't see why not. Let me ask my mom when she comes home from work later if it's ok. I'll call you later tonight, and thanks, Alex." Charlie had a grin on his face as he slowly hung up the phone.

That night at dinner, Charlie asked his mom if it would be alright to ride his bike across town to play with Alex and then to stay for dinner.

Charlie's mom's first response was to say no. She worried about Charlie riding his bike that far at night. Marie, who was listening to her brother's conversation, quickly added, "How about if I ride my bike with Charlie across town?"

Charlie's mom and dad looked at each other. Charlie's dad whispered something into his wife's ear, and she nodded her head up and down. "Ok, but be very careful you two," said their mom.

At about the same time, Alex was asking his father and mother permission to have Charlie over for dinner. While asking, Alex reminded his parents that just last week they had discussed the idea of having some of his classmates over to play. Alex's dad Thomas just smiled and looked over at his wife Hazel. "I guess he has us this time," said Thomas.

Hazel smiled at her son, "How does filet mignon with seasoned rice sound for dinner tomorrow night?"

"Great! Thanks mom, thanks dad," said Alex.

The next day Marie and Charlie rode their bikes over to Alex's house. "You weren't kidding about the house Alex lives in!" exclaimed Marie. "It's beautiful, and what an enormous yard they have. Boy, I bet you could fit a soccer field on his front lawn."

Marie and Charlie rode their bikes up the long driveway. Alex saw them from his bed-

room window and ran down the stairs and out the front door to greet them. Marie waved at Alex and turned to ride her old bike back home.

"Charlie, let me get my coat on, and we'll go jump our bikes down by the big old pond in my backyard," said Alex.

Charlie and Alex rode their bikes for over an hour when they heard Alex's mom calling them to come in for dinner.

At dinner Charlie kept looking around the dining room. He hadn't ever seen such a large dinner table as the one they were eating at. Thomas and Hazel couldn't believe their eyes at how much Charlie was enjoying his meal. They hadn't realized that Charlie had never eaten filet mignon before, until Charlie asked what kind of meat this was. "I have heard the expression that meat can melt in your mouth, but I never had a piece of meat like this. It really does seem to melt in your mouth," said Charlie. "Thank you so much for having me over for dinner."

Later that night after Marie rode back over

to bring Charlie home, Charlie told her everything about how great a house Alex lived in.

Chapter 3

The next day at school, Charlie and Alex were putting away their English books when Mr. Roberts announced a project he was assigning their class.

A low groan filled the room. Alex and Charlie looked at each other. Christmas break was only a few days away. Alex whispered to Charlie, "I can't imagine me doing school work over Christmas vacation. Doesn't Mr. Roberts have a heart?"

Before Charlie could answer Alex's question, Mr. Roberts began to speak. "Your assignment, class, will be for you to help someone at Christ-

mas. This person or persons that you help should be someone that does not live in your house. When you return from Christmas vacation, you can either hand in a two page report or give a five minute oral presentation to the class about what you did to help someone at Christmas. Now, class, does anyone have any questions about the assignment?"

Moments later the bell rang. Alex and Charlie picked up their books and trudged to their lockers. Twenty minutes ago many of the students in English class were day dreaming about Christmas vacation. Now many of the same students were trying to think of someone they could help at Christmas time.

A cold wind swept across the parking lot in front of the school. Charlie watched Alex get into his mother's Mercedes-Benz SUV and drive away. As Charlie started to walk home, a cold light rain began to fall. Usually the one mile walk from school passed rather rapidly. But today the walk seemed to last forever. The rain began to change to a type of hail, sleet, snow mixture. By the time Charlie got home, he was totally soaked. His hands were a bright red and felt numb. He slowly rubbed his hands together to get some circulation going in his fingers. After several minutes, Charlie lethargically began to remove his wet clothes.

All evening Charlie tried to get that cold feeling out of his of body. "Marie, how come we live in an old, drafty, cold house while Alex lives in a new, large, comfortably warm house?" inquired Charlie.

Marie smiled, "Charlie, why don't you stop feeling sorry for yourself and think about all the great things you have in your life."

"Like what?" exclaimed Charlie.

"For starters, like how lucky you are to have such a great sister," laughed Marie. "And remember what dad always said, just think of all the great things that you have to look forward to in life."

"Yea, you're right. I am pretty lucky to have such great parents," said Charlie.

Marie stood up, "What about how great a

sister you have?"

Charlie burst out laughing, "Yea, I guess you're ok, for a sister."

"Thanks a lot for the compliment. It's so nice that you could finally notice my fantastic traits, Charlie," smiled Marie.

Chapter 4

The rain turned to all snow as Charlie looked out his bedroom window. The weatherman said: "We might get up to two feet of snow with near blizzard conditions through-out the next day." Charlie had a hard time getting to sleep. He couldn't get the idea out of his head that he was poor. Until recently he had never thought about all the things he didn't have. Charlie has always been pretty much a happy-go-lucky kid. This feeling of jealously really bothered him.

The next morning, Marie ran into Charlie's bedroom. "No school, Charlie, we have a snow day."

Charlie rolled over and looked out his bedroom window. The snow was falling fairly hard. The window shook from the strong winds. The snow was coming down at a near horizontal angle. As Charlie scraped the frost from the inside of his window, he saw an old woman, Mrs. Arkwright, outside her front door trying to shovel a pathway to her mailbox.

Charlie got up out of bed and changed quickly into his play clothes. "Marie, how about coming outside with me and helping me shovel Mrs. Arkwright's front walkway?"

This was the last thing in the world that Marie was thinking of doing today. However, as she watched Mrs. Arkwright struggling to even make a dent in her shoveling of snow off her front sidewalk, Marie reluctantly got dressed to help Charlie.

Charlie and Marie put their heads down and with determination in their eyes walked over to Mrs. Arkwright's house. At least six inches of snow had fallen overnight. By the look of things, it appeared that the weatherman's prediction of at least one foot of snow would be correct.

"Hello, Mrs. Arkwright," yelled Charlie. "Marie and I will finish up shoveling for you."

Mrs. Arkwright turned to face both children. "No thanks. I can manage," exclaimed Mrs. Arkwright.

Charlie could see how difficult a time she was having shoveling the snow. Mrs. Arkwright's face was very pale with perspiration running down the sides of her face.

"I'm going to stop shoveling now anyway. It's no use shoveling the snow now. It is blowing right back onto the walkway as quickly as I shovel it away. I'll finish later after it stops snowing," said Mrs. Arkwright.

Mrs. Arkwright put her shovel by her front door and went inside. Looking out from her front window was a beautiful calico cat, Gabby, staring at them. Inside they could hear the barking of Mrs. Arkwright's yellow Labrador retriever, Sadie. Charlie and Marie slowly

turned away from the house and carried their shovels back to their own house.

Charlie and Marie shoveled their own front walkway for over thirty minutes before stopping. "It's no use, we'll have to do it later," yelled Marie. Charlie nodded his head in agreement and went inside.

"Why do you think Mrs. Arkwright didn't want us to help her shovel off her front walkway?" asked Charlie.

Marie thought about the question. Marie cleared her throat and whispered to Charlie, "I think it was because she is ashamed to ask for help."

"But why?" asked Charlie.

Marie looked into Charlie's big blue eyes. "Because she can't pay us to shovel her walkway," said Marie.

"But we didn't ask her to pay us. I just wanted to help her out. She looked like she was having so much trouble clearing a pathway herself," said Charlie.

"I know. But Mrs. Arkwright is a proud

woman. I don't think she wants us to know she can't afford to pay us for our work. I also think she doesn't know how to accept help from us," said Marie.

"I'm telling you, Marie, when it stops snowing, I'm going over to her house and clearing a pathway out to her mailbox. But I have to think of a way to do it without offending her. Do you have any ideas how I can do that?" asked Charlie.

Marie and Charlie spent the day sleigh riding and horsing around with their friends in the snow. After dinner Charlie noticed that the wind and snow had just about stopped. He asked his parents if he could go over to Mrs. Arkwright's house and shovel out her walkway of the nearly twenty inches of snow.

Charlie and Marie both went over with shovels in their hands. They were determined to clear a pathway from Mrs. Arkwright's front door to her mailbox out by the street.

The mailbox was nearly covered where the snowplows pushed the snow off their road.

Marie started to shovel out the mailbox, while Charlie started to clear a pathway from the street towards Mrs. Arkwright's front door. After nearly two hours of shoveling, Marie and Charlie had dug out the mailbox and most of the pathway to Mrs. Arkwright's front door.

With only ten more feet to go, the front door opened. A elderly woman looked out at them. Mrs. Arkwright was in a ruby red colored robe, with a rope tied tightly around her waist. "I told you kids not to shovel my walkway," her raised voice said.

"Please don't be mad, Mrs. Arkwright, we just wanted to help you out," said Charlie.

You could see tears welling up in Mrs. Arkwright's eyes. "Kids, I can't pay you right now, but I wish you hadn't done this."

"It's ok, we don't expect to be paid. As a matter of fact, we should really be the ones who owe you. We have to complete a school project, in which we are required to find someone who we can help at Christmas time. So really you are doing us the favor by allowing us to shovel your

walkway," explained Charlie.

Mrs. Arkwright pulled a tissue from her left pocket of her robe and wiped away several tears that had formed. "Can you kids come in for some hot chocolate and cookies?"

Before Marie could say "no thank you," Charlie nodded his head up and down and started for the front door. "Thank you for inviting us in," said Charlie.

Sadie, the yellow Labrador retriever, ran up to Charlie and Marie and started to give them some big wet licks across their hands. Gabby, the cat, meowed in the background and ran up to Marie and started to rub her head against Marie's leg.

Mrs. Arkwright smiled and had the kids take off their wet boots and coats in the foyer. She waved for the kids to follow her down a short hallway into a tiny kitchen. Within minutes the teakettle was boiling and hot chocolate was being made. On the kitchen table sat homemade chocolate chip cookies.

Charlie and Marie looked around at the inside of the tiny house. The house was fairly messy, with papers and things left everywhere. Mrs. Arkwright noticed their eyes looking around her house.

"I'm sorry the house is such a mess. I just can't seem to keep up with the housework and take care of the animals. I bet you can't guess how much Sadie weighs?" asked Mrs. Arkwright.

Marie looked at Sadie. "She is a big dog; I guess she weighs around 80 pounds."

Mrs. Arkwright laughed, "Not even close, Marie."

Charlie rubbed Sadie's ears, "I bet she weighs close to 100 pounds."

More laughter came from the elderly lady sitting across from them. "Would you believe she weighs 120 pounds? She really needs to be exercised more. But I can't walk her much any-more. She is just too big and strong for me. She darn near pulls me over when I do walk her, and with winter now here in full force, I'll be lucky to be able to walk her out to the street."

While Charlie and Marie were putting their boots and coats back on, Charlie had an idea. "Mrs. Arkwright, would it be ok if I came over and helped you out with Sadie and Gabby?" Before Mrs. Arkwright could answer, Charlie added, "I really need to get a good grade in Mr. Robert's English class. If you allow me to help you with some of your chores, you would be doing me a big favor."

"Since you put it that way, yes, Charlie, I would be very happy if you came over to help me out. Thank you!" exclaimed Mrs. Arkwright.

Charlie and Marie saw their dad outside shoveling their driveway. "One house shoveled out, and one to go," said Marie.

It took the three of them nearly two hours to clear away the snow from the driveway, sidewalk and mailbox. Charlie and Marie came into the house, exhausted. Marie turned to Charlie and said, "I hope we have a delayed opening at school tomorrow. I could really use a couple extra hours of sleep."

Charlie smiled and said, "I could use a couple extra hours of sleep, too. But I really can't wait until tomorrow when we have our Christmas party in Mr. Robert's room."

Chapter 5

Alex walked into the study where he saw his father working at his desk. "What are you doing, Dad?" asked Alex.

Thomas looked up from his checkbook and smiled. "I'm writing out some checks for some of the charities that your mother and I contribute to."

Alex thought about what his dad had just said. "Dad, I have an assignment in English, in which I am to help someone at Christmas. Is giving money to someone at Christmas time the same thing as helping someone at Christmas?"

Alex's dad, who was already starting to write

another check, stopped for a moment. Thomas looked across his desk at Alex and his glistening dark blue eyes. "Son, everyone can use money. So, yes, giving money to people less fortunate then ourselves is helping someone at Christmas."

A big broad smile came across Alex's face. "What's so funny?" asked Thomas.

"I was just thinking maybe I could give some money to the Santa Claus at the mall who rings his bell and has the large black pot hanging next to him," said Alex.

Thomas said, "I think I know who you are describing. I believe you're talking about giving money to the Salvation Army, who raises money every Christmas for the poor."

"That's it," said Alex.

Alex walked back up to his room and thought about the conversation he had just had with his dad. "I'll give fifty dollars to Santa Claus at the Salvation Army this weekend and I'll have half of Mr. Robert's assignment done," Alex whispered to himself.

Chapter 6

The next day Alex and his parents were taking a Sunday drive when he noticed his friend Charlie playing with a very large and rotund yellow Labrador retriever in the snow. Alex did not hesitate to ask his parents to drop him off to play with Charlie. Alex's dad said, 'Let's ask Charlie and his parents if it is okay for you to visit."

After getting permission to stay, Alex bolted out of the car towards Charlie. Charlie was surprised and had a look of disbelief on his face because he figured Alex had never been to this part of town.

Charlie yelled, " Come over, Alex, and play with me and my neighbor's dog, Sadie." Alex gladly accepted the offer and ran towards the large snow piles where Sadie and Charlie were playing.

"Whoa, Charlie, these piles of snow are monstrous! Did you shovel all this snow?"

"Yeah, my sister, Marie, and I shoveled our neighbor, Mrs. Arkwright's, walkway for her. I figured helping Mrs. Arkwright would be a good way to complete the project Mr. Robert's assigned us in English. We also take care of her dog, Sadie, and cat, Gabby, since the weather and her old age make it difficult for her to walk her dog in the snow and change the heavy litter box."

"Wow, that was a wonderful idea, Charlie," Alex responded. "I only gave the Santa Claus at the Salvation Army fifty dollars. Charlie, your gift is so much better than mine. Do you think I could help Mrs. Arkwright with you guys?"

"Of course, the more the merrier," replied Charlie.

"Great, when can I start?" asked Alex.

"How about right now. Helping out is a lot of fun and it makes you feel all warm and tingling inside," smiled Charlie.

Charlie was quite excited, but confused at first, that Alex was going to be helping him and his sister with Mrs. Arkwright and her pets. He thought fifty dollars was a great gift, but Alex made Charlie realize how special his gift really was because of his willingness to help.

Chapter 7

Charlie arrived home that night from walking Sadie and shoveling Mrs. Arkwright's driveway. He was exhausted. As Charlie plopped down on the sofa, his father walked into the room. "You look like you were in a twelve round fight and lost each round," laughed Charlie's dad.

"Well, you should see the other guy," replied Charlie, with a twinkle in his eye. Marie walked in as Charlie was finishing telling his father about what Marie, Alex, and he were doing for Mrs. Arkwright.

Charlie's dad gave Marie and Charlie a big hug. "I am so proud of you two, for helping Mrs. Arkwright with her pets and shoveling her driveway."

Hazel, Alex's mom, picked Alex up in front of Charlie's house. Alex slumped into the passenger's seat. "Is everything alright?" asked Hazel.

"Everything is fine," smiled Alex. "I'm just a little tired."

Alex lay on the couch in the family room watching television. He felt very good about what he had done today. A brouhaha erupted in the kitchen between Alex's mom and dad. "What's all the commotion?" asked Alex.

"Nothing too much," answered Thomas. "Your mother and I are debating what party we should attend for New Year's Eve!" he exclaimed.

"Remember, Thomas, it is important we keep everything in perspective. What parties we attend during the holiday season are very important in our social standings in the community," said Hazel.

Alex shook his head in disbelief. "I can't believe that the most important thing involving the Christmas season is which party you should attend."

"Young man, don't take that tone of voice with your mother," Thomas said in a raised voice.

Alex stood there with tears in his eyes. Hazel and Thomas looked at their son. Alex ran up the stairs and into his bedroom. Alex couldn't believe what had just happened.

He had felt so good about what he had done today. Now in just a few minutes his parents were able to drain all his happiness out of him.

Alex's mom and dad came upstairs together. "What's wrong, Son, I didn't mean to yell at you downstairs," apologized Thomas.

"It's not that, Dad. I'm just confused," explained Alex.

"What is it then?" asked Hazel.

Alex went on to tell his parents everything that Charlie, Marie, and he had been doing for

Mrs. Arkwright.

Hazel and Thomas looked into each other's eyes. Thomas turned and stared into his son's eyes. "Son, thank you for showing us an important lesson. You have demonstrated to both your mom and me that money is not always the key to happiness. I guess we have forgotten that money and social standing are fleeting commodities. The Christmas gift that lasts a lifetime is the gift of giving of one's self to help others. This is truly the best gift of all."

Bob Pryce is a graduate of Springfield College (B.S.), and Jersey City State College (M.A.). He has taught physical education and health for the past twenty-three years and has coached: track and field, soccer, softball, and basketball. This is his second novel. His first novel is entitled *Premonition*. He lives with his wife, Nancy, and four children in New Jersey.

Robyn Price is a senior in high school. She enjoys snowboarding, painting, and playing basketball. She plans to study art and journalism at the University of Montana.

Photograph of the authors by
Bobby Price

Cover Design by
Cherie Kocsis